# The Shutting Door

poems by

# Timothy Gager

Copyright © 2013 Timothy Gager

IBBETSON STREET PRESS
25 School Street
Somerville MA 02143

www.ibbetsonpress.com

ISBN 978-0-9678131-4-1

All rights reserved including the right to reproduce this work in any form except as provided by U.S. Copyright law. For information contact the publisher.

Author picture credit: Matthew Siditsky
Cover painting by Teisha Twomey
Book design by S.R. Glines
text: Gaudy Old Style
**titles: Gaudy**

# Dedication

To those who have helped me with my poetry and for those editors whom have published previous versions of these poems. To my children, Gabe and Caroline, whom I am always proud of the kind of human beings they have become and to the fellowship that allowed me to become a better person.

Special thanks to Teisha Twomey, whose patience, intelligence and overall knowledge of poetry further enhanced this manuscript and to Doug Holder, who published my first poem in 2002.

# Contents

| | |
|---|---|
| Dedication | v |
| Once We Were Friends | 3 |
| Ironing under an old Dusty Picture of a Wheat Field | 4 |
| Walking Out of the Woods | 5 |
| In My Hip High Waders | 6 |
| There's Sunshine when You Need It | 7 |
| Fourth of July, 2012 | 8 |
| Silent, Winter Remains | 10 |
| Reply to someone who said, "u owe me a poem, boy" | 11 |
| The Mistress through a Crystal Ball | 12 |
| The Lost | 14 |
| I have mostly Nightmares | 15 |
| What the Boy Prays For | 16 |
| The Shutting Door | 17 |
| Decomposition | 18 |
| Bar Stools | 19 |
| Missteps | 20 |
| The Photo Album | 21 |
| Quintessential Awkward Male Moment | 22 |
| The poems at my House | 23 |
| The Last Time in the Woods | 24 |
| Life of a Salesman | 25 |
| Sam Jesus in the Tub | 26 |
| On the Phone, In the Middle of the Night | 27 |
| You Knew Me Before | 29 |
| Meeting with Father Vincent | 30 |
| Often They Fall from the Sky | 31 |
| Chaos Boils under the Surface | 32 |
| After Hearing he had Six Months to Live | 33 |
| Scientific Purposes | 34 |
| Salmon Fishing in Alaska | 35 |
| January Poem | 36 |
| While I'm Driving Home | 38 |
| Definition of You | 39 |

| | |
|---|---|
| She is Lyrics which cause me to Rhyme | 40 |
| Seasonal Affective Disorder | 41 |
| How Grasshoppers Mate | 42 |
| What Do Men Want (in response to Kim A.) | 44 |
| Forgiveness | 46 |
| When I'm Drunk, I think about Phoenix | 47 |
| What Love Does | 48 |
| Love Affair | 49 |
| When you live by Yourself | 50 |
| All that we ate at Myrtle Beach | 51 |

# The Shutting Door

# Once We Were Friends

Lint in disheveled wool
two ingredients from a cold
rough mixture. Us,

becoming lisle, slurry
 too thick as thieves
we were robbing

infinite specks of meaning,
stealing how short time is;
sucking sweet air from hookah,

making a demarcation of opening
our arms—we're woven by love,
a single thread judders, unwraps,

warbles in unraveled sobs,
like an empty abode, endlessly
coming undone.

# Ironing under an old Dusty Picture of a Wheat Field

You imagine the wheat looks
like balloon headed girls

wearing checker board plaid
in searing sunlight, shade cooling

hot breeze; obedient wave, recalling
the goodbye to Mother as she left you

to your Aunt's care, don't forget her. Go
to the plains, venture into the field.

You're stuck, swamped in this city where cars
honked on dirty streets, muck sticks in gutters.

Your roof leaks during a rainstorm, you hold
an iron against your forearm until it's done.

# Walking Out of the Woods

there's a condom and ten suboxone
in the inside jacket pocket
but I won't use

either

it's been awhile
or there's a tree
standing in the

forest

gracefully not falling
except, through the branches,
there is brilliant

blue

look up,
god.
look up.

# In My Hip High Waders

On the shore,
across the river,
the beavers meet.

Their tails remind me
of spatulas flipping pancakes,
starting their day with mud

on one end, buck-teeth
choppers on the other.
No different today

than tomorrow but I need
a perfect cast; never fished
before; saw a picture of you

holding catch from hooked finger.
Hell, I've never thrown fly before,
attempted a roll cast, yet

knee high in the water
the sun to shows me trout.
They disappear into shadows.

# There's Sunshine when You Need It

New York City rains today.
People say, it may snow,
the weather's been bad
all year, at least, since
the last day of her life.

Wet cats and sick dogs,
sit on benches under newspapers,
their muscles clenched
in weak electrical currents
inducing dull pains in junkies.

I've offered a key to unlock
the lives jammed up.
I recall her door opened
to a bedroom with dead flowers
tipped on their sides. I remember:

scattered clothing, beer bottles
on scrap paper; roses given
by me before; the overdose,
the wilted joy from the world

says, "the weather's been bad
all year,' to which I say,
"True. It's been bad lately.
There's sunshine when you need it."

# Fourth of July, 2012

While coffee pot drips full,
a buckle of a belt, beats up my dryer.

I'm grateful for being home,
my children march in a parade downtown

My brothers and sisters visit
just twenty minutes up the highway,

two veins of road merge
their effort causing a slight tie-up

later, skipping the fireworks; I pay
homage to a sofa, not wasting life's time.

# Fresh Water

your silly hat
covered in a pattern
of lures and rainbow trout
sits crooked

on your tilted head
you wear a smile
and baggy fishing clothes.
The hat stays perched

when I unsnap your overalls,
yank your tank top
over your head~I swim
with you. We don't fish.

# Silent, Winter Remains

Sometimes, boots crunched
into snow, form a small puddle
inside the indented oval footprints,
sank down through crusted crystal,
where now there's only mud.

Twigs strained against the last storm
snapped, scattered on the ground;
gloveless hands tender to scrapes,
unable to avoid splitting,
never as strong as the branches.

Afterwards, in the shade, where snow
packed solid, you sit wanting
nothing. The forest empty, peaceful
palms raw and red, finally finding
something worth obliterating.

# Reply to someone who said, "u owe me a poem, boy"

Look around
there are poems everywhere.
There are ones in the weeds,
poems in the grass.

There are poems for lunch.
Somewhere there's someone
putting a chicken in every poem
a donkey, a monkey, a hundred cats.

I know there is a poem
about the time you snapped
my neck. Now I walk
taller but I didn't write that.

Instead, last night I wrote
on my way to the bottom of a bottle.
I re-wrote it again and again,
and then—I was finished.

# The Mistress through a Crystal Ball

I'm the woman waiting for
the husband to leave his marriage,
a picture in a marquetry, wishing
to pull myself out of veneer.

My lover says, his wife sees my face
in mahogany shelves, their pine
bookcase, oak arm
of the sofa. She rests

her dainty hands on there, covers
my image during a brief nap
after another fitful night.
Under the thin surface,

eyelids fluttering,
lips contorting,
in a series of arrant shapes
manifesting fear she could not control.

Mine, predeceasing his wife
before I could envision the future.
I visited a lying sibyl. She knew
truth, never exposing me a mark.

# Manomet Point

Standing halfway to your knees
the ocean, a vast bouquet, aerated—
as tides change, you push in, pull back;

lift salt water into your palm
funnel it through hands as big as
fishing boats off in the distance—

mermaids—for sure, you praise
God for such hope; so simple.

you find yourself joyous at pebbles
springing in somersaults;

the slick green seaweed rolling in
slow giggles which curl into laughter.

# The Lost

spoons, missing
from my house, taken
while you were here,
when I pretended people holed up
in bathrooms every hour
was something everyone did.

Coffee cup rings made
white stains on my table.
Cigarettes burned black lines
on my wood floor next to the sofa,
where you dropped them
from your fingers, one time,

your head wilted
into a plate of hummus. I hope
you recover with the bloom
of new days. I've filled mine
with quiet, like the roses,
no longer left to die.

# I have mostly Nightmares

You curl against me
the coastline, I wake to

your calf, it left a wrinkle
in my comforter;

a note; a funnel cloud,
destroyed everything,

you left the foundation,
the coffee maker brewing.

# What the Boy Prays For

He prays for
the two lobsters
left in the sink,
by his father.

The boy knows
there is no hope, even
when he pours water
over their heads

producing temporary comfort,
a twitch of worry--if he fills the sink
too far they might leap out.
He thinks of people forced to jump
off the top of burning buildings.

Streams of water deflect off
their brown bent shells. The ocean
as far away from them as any love
in the world from him. Any minute

his parents will be back; he surrenders
upstairs to his bedroom, hits his knees
in guilt, prays the lobsters won't feel
the pain of being boiled alive.

He'll strike a deal with God, if He exists
that prayers be answered conclusively,
he walks downstairs to find his mother
moving the lobsters to the freezer.

# The Shutting Door

We are solid oak doors that shut
on our past, close on dead mothers,
sons, daughters. These doors swell
often, won't open. One midnight

we walked towards woods, the moss
cold under our toes, as we were,
caught in the light for a moment;
a glimpse of half full. We are dim

lights on dark nights, sending out calls
to the wolves howling at the sun
because the moon hanging there,
yet never seems to hear them.

If I should need to step back to see
how you glow in this light,
illumination, I can be at one with that,
us, growing like violets in the dark

# Decomposition

Now it feels, I've subtracted my insides
as part of a more complex equation
I related to today, when I saw a possum

burrow into the anus of a dead cow
for food. I eat, gluttonously a sorted array,
quickly reach the end when starting with "A".

When starting with numbers things potentially
are infinite. I don't know figures too well.
I was at negative zero when you showed me

how algorithms worked. A blank slate—
plus a four dimensional dog, ate
 my chalk. Here's something I chew on:

When we go wrong, we curl together
like an annulus washer, convergence
a critical point if we calculate such conditions

as blood and maggots, things rotting
inside is what I know. Decomposition-
the way things completely break down.

# Bar Stools

Bar stools hold you the way
a woman might if she ever caught you

weeping, but you won't
let her grasp you in that

manner, yet, sometimes,
you fall off—

Bar stools are nothing
like all the women you list, lying

in bed, remembering each time
you've painted that ceiling.

# Missteps

When I raised my hand
told a gray room the reasons
I started drinking, I wanted
 to start again immediately.
Told people, whose faces looked like
The End of the World, the truth.

Then I told them I would pour a girl
I'd lusted after, down like whiskey,
her lovely legs spread
until they snapped,
so I could feel like I used
her, an orgasm, I gulped,

running down my neck
like streams of veins.
Oh, I said I never used dope,
when I asked her for it, nicely,
she said,  No, she would never

give it up, just got up, waltzed
out of my life. So I begged:
Please, God, stay with me tonight,
here in this church basement.
Please, I can't picture heaven.

# The Photo Album

A man and woman she knew embrace,
at the doorway of a new home.

An art opening she had years ago,
when she wore a dark dress,

matched her gray painted canvas;
all was stable in the frame.

There's the black Honda, with chrome
road wheels, stereo--a never ending road

which came crashing down, now
there's only a bus route close

to where she threw your hat. Another
photo, the two of us laughing

at a party that night I purred too close.
Ran away when she snapped that book shut.

# Quintessential Awkward Male Moment

A singular bead of sweat
traces my spine like a race track

when I plant down in front of her
"Do you want to get coffee sometime?"

She fidgets, looks down
"I don't think that's a good idea."

"Is it the caffeine?" I jest, always,
"if it's because you're seeing someone,

we're just having coffee—
if not we could get an espresso."

She grimaces the way one might
after a joke about cancer, says something

which may have been lost in a strong wind.
I stand like a small twig swaying.

# The poems at my House

My children are more than only words, rolled
together or random specks of dust flying
through amber light. It seemed fuzzy,
how they turned in flight to butterflies?

I wanted out of there. I'll stay
the caterpillar, I cannot change
the way my children leaned
over paper plates, ate watermelon,

the red juice ran down their bare legs,
spat out the seeds, as if they were
dirty things rising in an arc,
as far as they could go. Each moment

held it's sunlight on the lawn,
where my daughter ran,
thought poems were wishes
blown on dandelions,

"Be happy," she said,
handed me the limp stem
like a gift, or an obligation,
"Here".

# The Last Time in the Woods

She found the view of the treetops spectacular,
said, *You're not the only one who knows
about suicide*, turning over her wrists,
*The scars can hardly be seen.* Mine are

from twenty years ago, I found my friend
hung from a pipe, so I never looked back
or up again. In the woods it's clear
today, she saw the sky reaching

to heaven over strong branches.
Wiping twigs from her skirt, the needles
from her arms, asked *What do you think
God does?* I told her,

He could take on everything that
she didn't want. "Turn it Over", please,
as the saying goes, make love to me,
one more time. *I'm scared there is nothing;*

*afraid where we're heading,*
as we drove a few more hours, the car clung
to curves in the road, *You can drop me off
at my house.* This is where

He found her, propped up
with eyes closed, in a bathtub
filled with crimson water.
*She is with Me*, He calls. *She is safe.*

# Life of a Salesman

The Gentlemen's Club my client suggests
has dusty worn wood walls, an obstructive view of ladies
with saggy titties, corned beef asses slung over poles.
"Do you know anyone with cancer?" a question
in the pitch which once made a man cry.

"Huh," he grunts, while biting into a brown disc hamburger,
as I check his contact card which tells me, he's a plumber,
but this one a typo saying "Plumper". He pulls out
a five; his lunch grinds to a halt. He stops chewing,
his mouth open enough for me to see a piece of tomato.

For three hundred dollars he could upgrade to a package
which includes accidental death, disease, disability—
something I like to call the 3-Ds, straight forward, no shimmy,
butt slap or bending over, because I too bend over
each day, I conclude this is what's happening.

I lay my money down, the dancer crab walks,
loose flap of skin under her belly hanging,
straight at me, "I needz to pick up my kidz...
he's the only reason I do this." Gesturing sideways,
to the plumber, "Believe me, I understand."

# Sam Jesus in the Tub

On acid the orgy goers thought they were a tribe
worshipping a soapstone god with hymns
sounding more like Pink Floyd's Division Bell
Than Holy, Holy, Holy, Waters.

Violets overflow the bathtub like a womb with six knees
quadrangle of elbows, breasts, but one cock crowing,
bathed in wet vestments for the Almighty leading
to confessional prayers during this mass;
waiting and preparing for the Second Coming

# On the Phone, In the Middle of the Night

The sex is like a train passing—rushes through
my head, so out of me the sound came

a voice you described as Satan being drenched
with several pails of ice water. It's only good

as half a slice of pizza is. I still want a whole slice,
with everything. You say *That's something,*

*Do you want a dog?* I want a big quiet one
which doesn't bark all night, like my neighbor's

schnauzer whining and growling
like Cujo through the walls at 1 A.M..

My hands ball the sheets, wringing their necks until
death do us part? Once, your father choked your brother,

lifted him until he nodded off the wall,
years collapsing out of him—he never came back.

You say he never managed that wise-ass tact
which got him into trouble in the first place and

sometimes in the silence. a train's horn
sounds like a hymn for the lonely.

I can be there in an hour
if you keep talking like that.

## No Home Like Place

I have a strange sense of pride,
not from lack of foreplay
the way she's sore in the morning,

leaves need to be cleared
from the gutter, a chore I won't do
today. A stray cat cries outside;

It's not for nothing, she arrived only with
a set of clothes and a backpack.
Rescued by her father, his criticisms

sticking like flies on a no-pest strip,
a life as empty as the space
between this stanza



and the next one. I feed mangy animals
Raisin Bran, never thought the girl
fiddling with the pocketed keycard

from "The No Hope Hotel" would come.
Today she asks to send it back by mail.
It's the latest mistake she can conquer.

## You Knew Me Before

I was reincarnated
from an animal, a snake,
a pig, then lastly a bear.

You said you saw me
walking to the stream
pulling out raw salmon
with my teeth, jaws clenched,

sinking into the soft pink;
the spray from their guts
misted my face while I devoured
fermented berries until I laid

legs up, full bellied sleeping
in the sun after I roared,
raved, destroyed everything I touched,
my clothes wrinkled, shoes untied~

Remember how I held a knife and fork
like a hammer and chisel?
Look how I created something
beautiful out of rock.

# Meeting with Father Vincent

"Can you grasp the music of a thousand Gods?
*I* can," says Father Vincent. "False," is all I hear,
the aggregate of everyone's decomposition.

I believe in rusty trucks, feral cats and orphans.
People die for no reason, inherent wickedness
knows no spirit. The stone straight pastor tells me,

"There is hope in the unknown. I know,
we all decay in the ground, the same way,
then we're dust." I can't get a handle around that;

I don't carry a broom at all times. I am there,
a part of the "us". I believe in killer storms.
he says, there's no faith worse than death.

Trouble is, I can't believe in God without
swallowing pills. Men of the cloth have no idea,
what I can take; it's nothing they can prescribe.

# Often They Fall from the Sky

I want to save angels that attempt flight
with folded wings. They crash onto fields
heal imperfections, broken hollowed bones
lying on snapped, parted red cane.

I gathered one, tossed her in the back
of my pickup, head home to brush the dirt off,
sewed new pearly buttons on her dying gown.
The torn fabric once was spectacular.

A crowd of snowy winged angels
stood in formation, beat their wings
in my living room. I couldn't hold back
hands of clocks to prevent time's passing

or the breaking of gilded halos
from moving those angels, relentless
and never stopping to fly out of there.
They will never stop trying to fly.

# Chaos Boils under the Surface

When you tell me you don't have a home
I say, here take mine...take everything. Nothing

is left when you go; my hope
like a quilt which covered me

then turned down by my sofa which
left a note, that said, "I told you so,"

which it signed itself; before dancing away.
Now the wooden floor is cold and hard

as a winter lake against my bare legs.
I could settle into this block of ice.

You're happier when you're comfortable,
knowing *a watched pot never boils.*

You don't see this until later, the water
spews over the edge, violent as it is.

# After Hearing he had Six Months to Live

He thought about going on a road trip,
instead, he never left the house.
No longer able to negotiate miles
between gas stations and Waffle Houses.

Instead he never left the house,
the country too overwhelming,
between gas stations and Waffle Houses,
he'd aged twenty years,

in one month. Brittle, he never quit
reflecting, on Chevys and Marlboros,
inhaled the same way then exhaled,
when making love like gentle ringlets.

Reflecting on Chevys and Marlboros,
he couldn't make it past the sunsets,
when making love like gentle ringlets,
often, when he thought of the never.

He couldn't make it past the sunsets,
no longer able to negotiate miles,
often, when he thought of the never,
he thought about going on a road trip.

# Scientific Purposes

Your scent remains from today
when we were like an isotherm
which took the longest distance
from two points: A drive to

an empty parking lot to kiss,
then found a Days Inn to watch TV,
conducting experiments, concluding
our hypothesis kicked butt of mere supposition

# Salmon Fishing in Alaska

They passed out flyers on campus, Ten grand
to work with experienced fisherman, so we,
kid drunks said, north to Alaska for adventure
money and to sing, *The Wreck of the Edmund Fitzgerald.*

Day One, a bad omen, Cappy, the skin on his face
a relief map of experience said, welcome boys,
we'll supply you with the beer...that first day,
five of us college boys went through two cases

but only a few people blamed us, except Cappy
whose little speech about too many fish reeled in
could sink the boat, or one shoe-lace caught a net
could toss you, or lack of attention will take a few fingers.

Risk takers? We were more like the dogs, cats, and ducks,
from the Little Red Hen. Who will cask the net?
Not I, said the duck, Who will store the fish? Not I.
Who will sit on the deck with a beer, cash the check?

Yes, yes, we will do that until we got cut off,
Day Two, no beer, a contract broken. Why/
Maybe Rob's sustained horror movie scream
when the first haul flopped on the deck.

Maybe Teddy pushing Cappy against the cabin wall,
"I don't think this is working out," Teddy yelled after
rations were removed, maybe, Jerry was throwing up
over the starboard side, with nothing to do with sea legs.

By Friday Cappy asked us to move on, no goodbyes,
no, *Fellas it's been good to see ya, To know ya,*
only good to Fire ya, with a look of disgust,
as we went to get wrecked.

# January Poem

Winter's trees unadorned
reach towards the mountains,
up to a low-lit sky's

empty embrace,
as solid as spit on twigs,
an unreliable love nest

with attached snow
clinging to a cruciform,
earth's meager prayer,

unveiling your brittle state:
you haven't slept in weeks
when a pale white glossing aged

you ten years during the time
a painted wall turns
itself dull to bright.

# Back in Boston

A torrential downpour every day:
striking the sidewalks and roads

that seem more curved than before,
falling loud in brutal run offs, over which

I hear bits of homeless conversation
"A standing poodle is a substantial dog."

The force of this storm
hits a woman's plastic bag,

which covers a wedding dress,
tightly like a snare drum.

Another man turns to his wife,
says, "I hope this stops soon,"

but she can't know he's saying,
"I need you in my life,

I love you," as a door
held open for her falls

closed like the weather,
that never seem to change.

# While I'm Driving Home

Your boyfriend Chuck bounces a basketball
out the window from the backseat of the moving car

Chuck's no Pistol Pete Maravich, more like slick
Willie, but I've already had that chat with him.

Try to stay as clean as she, don't shoot behind her back;
but he popped a Subutex into his mouth, crunched it

like Pez and laughed. Now he dribbles in the back
as she sits soaking wet in the front seat after we sang,

and danced in the rain, my fault, you got
drenched when I couldn't find the car

in Kenmore Square, we walked down the wrong street,
ended up in Back Bay, the weather not cooperating

not bothering to warn me, it's a waste to find your way,
since I've never danced like Gene Kelly, especially

when I kicked at some puddles, shot some spray, came
on with the rain, had a smile on my face, when Chuck

got splashed in the face...he will never stop dribbling.
He continues, again and again, turns the ball over.

# Definition of You

sweet you.
open me up completely
my bare bones visible,
rest between my ribs, you
and me, wired together.
our brains in synch, soft brush
strokes on canvas painted
wild flowers emerge
in bright color exploding
through the snowy crust.
Winter is finally averted.

# She is Lyrics which cause me to Rhyme

My lover.
A perfect poetic verse, she's
my moon who blushes and swoons,
a perfect song for two,
I'm Johnny, she is June.

When she walks beneath
giant sunflowers, they tremble,
allow for an impasse, as she only brushes
gently against their naked stems,
moving between them the way a tiny leaf,

finds its way down a stream. She is
brightly painted, stunning, obscene
she is what filters down through
crisscrossed branches,
who makes herself seen

as a light
only to me
only to me.

My lover is
a perfect poetic verse, she's
my moon who blushes and swoons,
a perfect song for two,
I'm Graham, she is Emmy Lou.

# Seasonal Affective Disorder

every year, the same thing
same season
same damn routine
same autumn,
a handful of tiny white pills
washed down by whiskey
erases last night

instead I don't wake
with a thought of placing a gun
against my temple how cool
it would feel— the air heavy

hanging from a rafter.
instead, I read the paper
'bout a man on a highway.
who opened his car door
walked out, straight into
an 18 wheeler, it's what he wanted
he just wanted to walk out..

# How Grasshoppers Mate

They have individual songs for each other,
the product of stridulation  and chemistry.
At first the male attracts the female—
waves brightly colored wings, emits
external hormones to hypnotize her.

The tiny, wingless grasshopper of Costa Rica
Has a brilliant green body~glimmering
gold gilded accents on its head,
thorax and genitals. The male drums
it's hind legs on its preferred plant food.

Mine is lobster but I'd never attempt to strike a beat
on its shell except the sound of nut crackers
when I crack it open, The hum when I suck down the meat.
Eating is not a part of our elaborate courtship ritual
of verses and voids of seeing each other

singing Bonnie and Clyde, Jay Z and B,
are you ready T? Our chemistry, so many hours
in a day. Mating occurs when the male lights
on the female's back, lasting anywhere from
an hour to well over twenty-four.

# Zombie Zeus

He makes love to her brain, eats her
like a cannibal, swallows her

just so the baby can be born
out of his forehead, the push

begets a scar; the gash sutured,
new memories in bed. Asleep,

Zeus feels his face in her jaw, skull\
throbbing. People are always talking

about Zeus. Zeus, Zeus, Zeus.
What was Metis prior to her

fateful swallowing? They said
she'd had excellent taste

# What Do Men Want (*in response to Kim A.*)

I want a woman in a red dress.
flimsy and cheap, too tight,
and want her to wear it
until I can tear it off her.
I want a case of cheap beer,
in a Styrofoam cooler, sweat
beading on the bottle
the same way it forms
on my back before
it soaks through my shirt.
I want that woman
to peel off her dress
and dance naked,
while handing me scotch
when it's time to move on.
I want her to understand
when all I want to do is lie
in bed, smoke cigarettes
while she drapes herself
over my ankles. I want the softness
of her red camisole massaging
the tops of my feet and I want
the drinks to be handy
so we won't have to move,
except into each other
the pure harshness all poured down
my throat soothed
by the velvety texture of her
panties, and I want to pull them
to the side, check what's underneath.

I want a woman who will make me feel
that I'm perfection in a vessel,
who'll think, my paycheck is larger
than I know it is. Who'll tell me, my dick
is larger as well. I want to be the only man
badass enough to drive a rusted out car
out there to her, not worry about the weather
report or the floorboard leaking.
There'll still be a "chance of blowjob"
so my dark clouds don't matter
by the time her thighs start pumping
all the sunshine out of me
so hot the world burns, hotter than hell.

# Forgiveness

Our terseness flaps
like a torn wing of a butterfly
that beating in cupped hands
trying to soar away, please
this is not a healing place
so, I place you in my shirt pocket
close to my heart 'till the rain
stops. Later, you find
a warm open anemone
to settle down on

# When I'm Drunk, I think about Phoenix

The time I just drove there
with an American Express
in my pocket but no coin
for a pay phone I found

by accident, a sunny bar
with green velour drapes frosted
with dust, must be dumb luck
Ma Bell's out of order, when I flushed

the change lever the coins poured out
like this story: just me
and the bartender; lonely, she laughed
as if I was a lottery winner

when I paid for two Budweisers
with dimes, she smiled, said,
a few more pulls and tugs
here, I'd never want to leave.

# What Love Does

Stirs chemicals in our brains
causing addictions more advanced
than seen in the grappling world of animals
whose natural habitat isn't a crowded bar,

a brightly lit trolley or supermarket.
A spectral bat doesn't care who browses
the fruit or crisp vegetables alongside it.
Yet lovers, it is argued remind us

of our parents or ourselves. Researchers
conclude we all strive for incest
perhaps we should go fuck ourselves.
(which is backed up somewhere with data)

Try counting pheromones with a slide rule,
calculate the folklore quotient of an aphrodisiac.
A Spanish fly is not a fly, it's made of crushed beetle
parts. We don't measure love in a bucket, only know

the lightness of touch, the warmth of their
body in increased degrees, the finite
number of each infinite laugh. Every time
oxytocin is released, our bond becomes stronger.

# Love Affair

after a split of wine
a hard-boiled egg
and a mint, I call
to ask "cool?"
"are we?" she says

we sit on the fence
as clear a comparison
of Bob Dylan to Pavarotti
singing *Nessun Dorma*

# When you live by Yourself

You can bench press
your weight in quietness
gets so you talk to your cats
but they won't say
"I love you," back.

You listen to the world
through those feeling-sorry-
for-myself songs, you wish
you never played
over and over again.

## All that we ate at Myrtle Beach

Was bad times at Grammas' Buffett,
each pan tasted of greasy grease.

Gramma did all that deep fried
from frozen food thang. We wondered

where canned corn acquired an oil slick
if Gramma were alive, might we  go

to the Nursing Home, complain: terrible
home cooking passed to each generation.

You imaged the waitress was her granddaughter,
you hated her because we stayed sick in bed

the rest of the day, so many better things
to do than channel changing without touching,

each hour we sweated her out, but
the documentary on bulimia was really great.

Many of these poems appeared as previous versions in some very fine journals. To view and support them please visit the "PUBLISHED WORK" tab at www.timothygager.com.

© 2013 Matthew Siditsky

"THE SHUTTING DOOR" is Timothy Gager's tenth book. His fiction and poetry have appeared over 250 times in literary journals and he has been nominated for the Pushcart Prize nine times. Also, his work has been read on National Public Radio.

Timothy was formerly the Fiction Editor of The Wilderness House Literary Review, the founding co-editor of The Heat City Literary Review and he has hosted the successful Dire Literary Series in Cambridge, Massachusetts every month for the past twelve years. Timothy, with Doug Holder, is the co-founder of Somerville News Writers Festival. A graduate of the University of Delaware, Timothy lives in Dedham, Massachusetts and is employed as a social worker.

# More Praise for Timothy Gager

Worldly, witty, and often satirical, these poems also have a tender side, a feeling of loss and longing, a sense of thwarted hopes and dreams. It is as if the poet has glimpsed something wondrous and maybe all-important just beyond a door that is closing. What did he see in there? Was it his beloved, or the remnants of love grown cold? Was it the hem of God, or the remnants of a faith no longer held? Was it a little bit of truth and beauty mixed together, or was it the death of either, or both? Questions on this order are at the heart of these poems, and the glimpses of the answers are real enough to help us keep going.

Fred Marchant, author of The Looking House

The Shutting Door is gritty, captivating book that immediately pull you in and doesn't let go. Tim Gager writes through the lens of a damaged angel, someone who has seen forgiveness from all sides. The result is wondrously eloquent, giving us these beautiful, dangerous, arresting poems about what it means to be human. Gager's poems "never stop trying to fly,"

~January Gill O'Neil, author of Underlife, Executive Director of Mass Poetry Festival

"The Shutting Door" is unflinchingly honest and deeply personal, with a gentle sense of melancholy offset by the occasional touch of gallows humor. These poems shift effortlessly from meditations on nature, tales of love found and love lost, and astute observations on the human condition. Timothy Gager mines gems of truth from the plain soil of ordinary life.

~Charles Coe, author of All Sins Forgiven: Poems for My Parents

www.ingramcontent.com/pod-product-compliance
Lightning Source LLC
Chambersburg PA
CBHW020022050426
42450CB00005B/605